Internet Guide
for Criminal Justice
Second Edition

Christina DeJong
Michigan State University

Daniel J. Kurland

THOMSON
™
WADSWORTH

Australia • Canada • Mexico • Singapore • Spain • United Kingdom • United States

Printed in Canada

4 5 6 7 06 05

ISBN: 0534-57263-4

For more information about our products, contact us at:
Thomson Learning Academic Resource Center
1-800-423-0563

For permission to use material from this text, contact us by:
Phone: 1-800-730-2214
Fax: 1-800-730-2215
Web: www.thomsonrights.com

Asia
Thomson Learning
5 Shenton Way #01-01
UIC Building
Singapore 068808

Australia
Nelson Thomson Learning
102 Dodds Street
South Street
South Melbourne, Victoria 3205
Australia

Canada
Nelson Thomson Learning
1120 Birchmount Road
Toronto, Ontario M1K 5G4
Canada

Europe/Middle East/South Africa
Thomson Learning
High Holborn House
50-51 Bedford Row
London WC1R 4LR
United Kingdom

Latin America
Thomson Learning
Seneca, 53
Colonia Polanco
11560 Mexico D.F.
Mexico

Spain
Paraninfo Thomson Learning
Calle/Magallanes, 25
28015 Madrid, Spain

CONTENTS

PREFACE

The Internet has changed dramatically since the first edition of this guide in 1997. Since that time web pages have become sophisticated and streamlined, with more information than ever available at the click of a finger.

Much of the information presented in this book will be very useful for supplementing material in your criminal justice courses. In addition, it is fair to say that a good deal of the material presented within may not be very conducive to study (listening to Internet radio, perhaps, or finding an off-topic chat room). Some have called this the beauty of the Internet—it contains the ability to educate as well as waste tremendous amounts of our time.

Chapter 1 contains Daniel Kurland's concise and informative description of Internet services is retained in this second edition. It provides an excellent introduction to the components of the Internet and how they are used.

Christina DeJong (formerly Polsenberg) adds important information about using the Internet in undergraduate education, and then specifically for criminal justice research in the chapters following. Chapter 2 covers information sources on the Internet, and how to supplement your criminal justice education online. Chapter 3 contains important information on finding data sources online, and how to find information and statistics to enhance papers and reports for class. Chapter 4 focuses on careers in criminal justice, and how students can use the Internet to both find career opportunities as well as package themselves for the job market.

Finally, an Appendix for instructors has been added to showcase some of the ways in which the Internet can be used to enhance the classroom environment.

The authors are grateful to several people for contributing to the content of this book. Stephen Schwitzer was an indispensable asset to the evolution of this text. His Internet expertise was exceptionally helpful, and he helped to correct several errors in the text (any that remain are the sole responsibility of the authors).

Finally, while writing this text we were able to "pick the brains" of several members of the Usenet community. They helped to keep us informed on the latest software applications and their availability, and were more than willing to have their (virtual) pictures taken for several screen shots in the book. We are indebted to Nick Simino, "Debz", Alexander Moon, John Iwaniszek, Erica Sadun, Rick Savoia, Tyler Trafford, Graham Thurlwell, "Thinkum", Tim Weaver, Mark Morrison, and "netmamma" for their willingness to help make this text even more helpful for the naïve reader.

Chapter 1

What is the Internet?

The Internet has been portrayed with a variety of images. Allusions are made to road systems ("The information superhighway"), Star Trek adventurers ("Internauts in cyberspace"), and to a world community (the "electronic global village").

Initially, the Internet might best be seen within the historical development of human communication. At heart, the Internet is merely a new stage in humanity's ongoing attempt to meet people, exchange information, and explore the world of ideas. But it is also more than this.

The Internet is at once a mailbox, a research tool, a vehicle of commerce, and a medium of entertainment. You can send a letter to a colleague in Japan, check the score of the last Wizards game and the progress of a Senate Bill, order a present for Aunt Harriet's birthday, listen to a sample track from a new CD, and find a recipe using avocado for supper tonight.

The Internet and the College Student

Public discussion focuses on the Internet as a burgeoning electronic mall for cyber-consumerism and multimedia entertainment. For students and professors, the Internet has other purposes.

The Internet offers a broad array of academic and academic-related resources:

- Professional and governmental archives and databases
- On-line journals

- Access to commercial databases and abstract services.
- Professional discussion via newsgroups, mailing lists, and discussion groups
- Academic and public library catalogs
- Grant listings and deadlines
- Directories of researchers and research projects funded by the federal government
- Conference announcements and calls for papers
- Academic, government and industry job announcements
- Faculty biographies and university course descriptions
- Educational and other software.

In a broader vein, you can find the latest ferry schedule for Martha's Vineyard, browse advertisements for rafting trips, and download guides to doing your taxes.

Professors have used E-mail to post answer keys and grades, course organization software (such as Blackboard) to give exams and quizzes on-line, and the World Wide Web to offer problem sets, interactive demonstrations, and supplementary course materials.

For graduate students and researchers, then, the Internet is an important resource for communicating with the community of scholars, for accessing sophisticated databases, for sharing information, and for investigating potential teaching/research programs.

For the undergraduate, the initial use of the Internet may be as a tool for communicating with the professor and other students. A secondary use may be to access information and discussion of real-world applications and policy issues. If you want to learn a particular discipline, study the textbook. If you want to review government documents, or discussion on issues within that discipline, surf the Internet.

Getting Connected

To obtain telephone service, you must subscribe to a telephone company. To access the Internet, you must connect to an Internet provider—a host or gateway providing an on-ramp to the Internet.

When a host computer offers a specific service, it is referred to as a server in a client-server relationship.

Most colleges and universities provide some form of Internet access. At one extreme, access may be limited to specific computers in a computing center or laboratory. At the other extreme, wireless access may be available campus-wide.

In general, Internet access will entail one of three options:
- Direct linkage to the university network
- Telephone access via modem to the university network
- Telephone access via model to a local or national commercial provider

The preferred method of on-line access for college students is the University network, since this is often offered free to charge to students, staff, and faculty. However, Internet services are available from commercial on-line services such as America Online or the Microsoft Network for a monthly service fee. Contact your computer center to assess your options.

The World Wide Web

When people hear the word "Internet," they often think of the World Wide Web. Indeed, the terms Internet and World Wide Web have become practically interchangeable. There is, however, more to the Internet than just the Web (as it is commonly called). This section will provide an overview of the World Wide Web, and later we'll discuss some of the additional features of the Internet.

Of all the aspects of the Internet, the World Wide Web (WWW) has evoked the greatest hyperbole. Laurie Flynn, in The New York Times, referred to it as "an electronic amalgam of the public library, the suburban shopping mall and the Congressional Record," while Peter H. Lewis, in the same newspaper, referred to it as "a time-sucking black hole... a speed trap on the data highway, a Bermuda Triangle in the information ocean, the junk food aisle in cyberspace's digital supermarket."

The World Wide Web is a means of accessing files on computers connected via the Internet. The World Wide Web is not a physical place, nor a set of files, nor even a network of computers. The heart of the World Wide Web lies in the protocols that define its use. Yet it is the appearance of the Web that is most striking.

Uniform Resource Locators (URLs)

Other than for e-mail transactions, most Internet activity involves accessing files on remote computers. Each file or directory on the Internet (that is, on a host computer connected to the Internet) can be designated by a Uniform Resource Locator (URL).

URLs indicate:
- the program for accessing a file,
- the address of the computer on which a file is located,
- the path to that file within the file directory of that computer, and,
- the name of the file or directory in question.

Thus URLs have the form *protocol://IP Address/file path/filename*. Consider an example:

http://www.fbi.gov/ucr/ucr.htm

The first part of the address—*http://*—specifies the means of access, here Hypertext Transfer Protocol, associated with the World Wide Web. The address immediately following the double slash—*www.fbi.gov*—indicates the address of the computer (server) to be accessed.

Terms following single slashes—here, */ucr*—indicate progressively lower subdirectories on the server. And finally a specific file name—*ucr.htm*—is recognizable by the period within the name and the .htm ending indicating HyperText Markup Language—and is, again, associated with the World Wide Web (URLs are indicated with italics throughout this text). HTML files also use the extension .html following the file name.

There are URLs for all Internet protocols (telnet, FTP, http) as well as for e-mail addresses, file locations and newsgroups. For more information on URLs, see "A Guide to URLs," *http://www.netspace.org/users/dwb/url-guide.html*.

Internet Addresses

Each account on the Internet is assigned a unique address. House addresses divide the world into physical regions: houses on streets, in towns, in cities. Internet addresses indicate computers on networks within networks.

Each level of the network is referred to as a *domain*. Thus the computer running the Web site of the National Center for Supercomputing Applications (NCSA) at the University of Illinois at Urbana-Champaign (UIUC) has the address *http://www.ncsa.uiuc.edu*. This is the Internet way of indicating a particular computer at a particular center (ncsa) within a larger university network (uiuc). The final abbreviation indicates the nature of the account, here an educational institution (edu).

The most common final domain extensions include:

edu	educational institutions
gov	government institutions
com	businesses or Internet service providers
biz	businesses
info	information sites
name	web sites for individual people
mil	military sites
net	organizations involved in the Internet
org	private organizations, frequently non-profit

Foreign addresses include an additional two-letter country abbreviation at the end, e.g., *http://manet.ora.nsysu.edu.tw*, the address of the Web site of the National Sun Yat Sen University in Taiwan. The listing of current domain endings for all countries is available at: *http://www.iana.org/cctld/cctld-whois.htm.*

All domain addresses have a numerical Internet Protocol (IP) address equivalent. IP addresses consist of four numbers separated by dots. The notation 141.142.20.50 is the same address as *ftp://ftp.ncsa.uiuc.edu.*

The look! Each Web site opens with a home page, "a combination frontispiece, greeting room, table of contents, hub, and launching pad," in the words of Michael Neubarth, editor-in-chief of Internet World.

A Web page has all the aspects of sophisticated desktop publishing: diverse typefaces, charts and forms, icons and integrated graphics. Sound and movies can even be integrated into the presentation. Recent increases in computer speed have spawned applications utilizing real-time sound and 3-D or virtual reality graphics.

The main FBI Web page (*http://www.fbi.gov*) appears as:

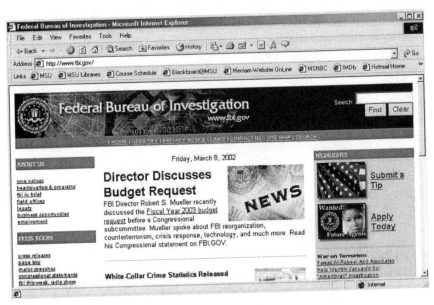

What's behind it all: Hypertext. The World Wide Web is based on the notion of links within hypertext pages. In hypertext, key concepts and ideas are linked to the address of related material. Links within the discussion are indicated by highlighted terms, icons, or simply locations on the page called hotspots. Click on a hotspot, and you access the linked item, be it another Web page or any one of a number of the other Internet services. Footnote numbers can provide direct access to the original sources. Links can be inserted into maps and drawings. You can click on a room in a blueprint and see a photograph of that room.

The overall effect is not unlike reading an encyclopedia with the ability to snap your fingers to instantly shift to another page, another book, or even a phonograph or slide projector! You do not need to follow a predetermined sequence of ideas. You can branch off as your interests dictate.

Hypertext transfer protocol (HTTP). Hypertext linkage is accomplished with Hypertext Transfer Protocol (HTTP), the main operating system of the World Wide Web—hence the URL notation *http://.* This protocol contains the instructions to connect to a remote computer, request a specified document, receive the document, and sever the connection.

Hypertext markup language (HTML). The coding of a World Wide Web page is done with Hypertext Markup Language (HTML). Just as a word processor inserts codes to indicate fonts and font sizes, paragraph breaks and boldface, so HTML inserts tags or elements to accomplish the same effects. The resulting format is seen only when the page is read by a Web browser.

Consider the main page of the New York City Police Department, located at *http://www.nyc.gov/html/nypd/home.html:*

The following is the first part of the HTML document underlying the NYPD home page (We have edited the HTML to fit our page size—the entire HTML document is 27 pages long!). Addresses are indicated in uniform resource locator (URL) notation. On-screen text has been marked in boldface to distinguish it from the hypertext markup language coding. Hyperlinks, indicated on screen by a contrasting color, are indicated here in italics.

```
<!doctype html public "-//w3c//dtd html 4.0 transitional//en">
<html>
<head>
```

<TITLE>NYPD - Official New York City Police Department Web Site</TITLE>

```
<BODY leftmargin=0 rightmargin=0 marginwidth=0 marginheight=0
topmargin=0 text="#000000" link="#000000" vlink="#3333CC"
alink="#FF0080">
```

```
<center>
<!-- ImageReady Slices (1home-banner-pc.psd) -->
<TABLE WIDTH=720 BORDER=0 CELLPADDING=0 CELLSPACING=0>
<TR><TD COLSPAN=2>

<A HREF="./html/brass/pc.html">
<IMG SRC="./pix/3100/1home-banner-pc_01.gif" WIDTH=130
HEIGHT=31 BORDER=0 ALT="Raymond W. Kelly, Police
Commissioner"></A></TD><TD ROWSPAN=4>

<IMG SRC="./pix/3100/1home-banner-pc_02.gif" WIDTH=590
HEIGHT=120 ALT="New York City Police Department"></TD>
</TR><TR><TD>

<A HREF="./html/brass/pc.html"><IMG SRC="./pix/3100/1home-banner-
pc_03.gif" WIDTH=53 HEIGHT=27 BORDER=0 ALT="Biography of
Police Commissioner Raymond W. Kelly"></A></TD><TD
ROWSPAN=3>

<A HREF="./html/brass/pc.html"><IMG SRC="./pix/3100/1home-banner-
pc_04.gif" WIDTH=77 HEIGHT=89 BORDER=0 ALT="Raymond W.
Kelly, Police Commissioner"></A></TD></TR><TR><TD>

<A HREF="../mail/html/mailnypd.html"><IMG SRC="./pix/3100/1home-
banner-pc_05.gif" WIDTH=53 HEIGHT=30 BORDER=0 ALT="Email the
Police Commissioner"></A></TD></TR><TR><TD>

<IMG SRC="./pix/3100/1home-banner-pc_06.gif" WIDTH=53
HEIGHT=32></TD></TR></TABLE>
<!-- End ImageReady Slices -->
```

(Note from authors: HTML continues until the end of the document...)
</html>

Notice that an HTML document, unlike a document produced with a word processor, is in plain ASCII text. The result is a universally accessible page that can be read by browsers using any operating system, whether Windows, Macintosh, or UNIX.

For discussion of Hypertext Markup Language, see A Beginner's Guide to HTML (*http://www.msg.net/tutorial/html-primer.html*), HTML help (*http://www.obscure.org/~jaws/htmlhelp.html*), or the Almost Complete HTML Reference at (*http://www.computronics.be/courses/htmlcourse/otherinfo/specs.html*).

Web browsers. The World Wide Web is accessed with programs called browsers. The browser Mosaic (by the NCSA) is to a great extent responsible for the initial explosion of the World Wide Web; Microsoft Internet Explorer and Netscape Navigator have since become the standard for most users.

A Web browser is in reality an HTML reader. A browser reads the HTML code indicating such attributes and bold <BOLD>, a list of items <LI>, or links <A HREF=>. Outdated browsers cannot read newer code, and users can control some attributes, such as the size and font of the type. Thus, while all browsers can read any HTML page, any single page can look different on different browsers.

Web browsers open on a default home page. It may be the home page of your Internet provider, the home page of the browser program, or any page that you have designated. Utilizing Hypertext Transfer Protocol, Web browsers access Web locations, follow hypertext links, and create an ongoing history of the sites visited in your travels.

Constructing your own home page. Anyone can create a home page to use as an opening page with his or her browser. No programming experience is required, and most word processing programs (such as Corel WordPerfect or Microsoft Word) will save documents in HTML format for easy upload via FTP to a Web server.

There are many free services on the Internet that will provide you with free space for a Web page. You can check with your college or university, or find a site that allows users to have a limited amount of free space for Web pages, such as Geocities (*http://yahoo.geocities.com*). If you pay for Internet access, you will likely be given some space for your own Web pages.

Communication and Collaboration on the Internet

E-mail: The Internet as Post Office

Academic research relies on the efforts of a community of scholars. Central to this effort is communication. The major use of the Internet—by scientists as well as by others—is electronic mail and a number of other communications services based on electronic mail.

What is e-mail? In many ways, e-mail is truly revolutionary. E-mail travels anywhere in the world in seconds instead of days (is it any wonder that regular mail is commonly referred to as "snail mail?"). You can send a document thousands of miles for the price of the phone call to your Internet provider (or free, if directly connected). Having trouble getting through to someone on the phone? E-mail. When you can't get past a secretary? E-mail. Tired of waiting on hold? E-mail.

In other respects, little has changed. You still have to have something to say to someone, and you still have to know that person's address. There is still the excitement of discovering that you have mail—and still the nuisance of wading through junk mail.

The Internet delivery system can overcome many problems, but it is not foolproof. Lines may be down or computer systems may be out. Excessive traffic may slow access to a particular location—and even the Internet cannot surmount an incorrect address. E-mail reports back unknown addresses and problems with delivery, but regular mail is more forgiving of simple errors in addresses.

Using e-mail. E-mail programs are part word processor, part mailbox, and part file organizer. With almost all you may
- List mail received and mail sent
- Read or delete an item from the list of documents received
- Print or save a document as a file
- Store frequently used names and addresses
- Automatically attach signatures at the end of letters
- Send replies, with portions of the original message in the reply
- Forward mail by simply readdressing it
- Attach other files to mail

- Send a document to any number of people at once.

This final feature facilitates the postal equivalent of the traditional telephone tree and enables a number of additional services considered below.

E-mail addresses. Domain addresses are equivalent to street addresses. But street addresses alone are not sufficient to designate the location of a specific individual. Many individuals may live in the same house with the same street address. Similarly, a number of users may access the Internet from the same host, and hence from the same Internet address.

For this reason, the e-mail address of an individual user consists of a username and domain address: user@domain, pronounced "user at domain." The username and domain address together make up a complete Internet e-mail address.

Finding addresses. Since there is no definitive Internet, there is no definitive directory of Internet names and addresses. The best way to learn a person's e-mail address is still to call the person on the telephone, or ask someone else. If that fails, you can try a number of search programs examining portions of the system. Try Switchboard (*http://www.switchboard.com*) or a search engine that uses a number of other sites to search, such as *http://www.search.com*.

Mailing Lists and Discussion Groups: The Internet as Bulletin Board, Bull Session, and Party Line

Mailing lists. The same process by which a single e-mail message can be directed to another person can be used to distribute documents—almost as with traditional mailing lists.

Individuals subscribe by e-mail and receive material periodically via e-mail. (Nonsubscribers can usually request individual items from the mailing list via e-mail, although much of this is now available on Web sites). Since all such mailing list activities involve e-mail, the only software required is an e-mail program.

In many instances, subscription mailing lists are administered by a computer. The first such program was LISTSERV, giving rise to the name listservers. Similar programs go by the names majordomo, MAILSERV, and listproc.

Server computers automatically read and respond to requests to start, stop, or pause subscriptions. Most such programs oversee more than one list at a single site. A sure sign that a mailing list is administered by machine is that the contact address refers to one of the above programs. Listservers commonly archive correspondent in log files that can be retrieved by e-mail.

Administrative tasks are usually accomplished by single-word commands—commands that vary with the listserver program involved. An e-mail letter to a listserver with the single word help in the body of the letter will usually evoke a reply with a list of appropriate commands.

Professional groups, on-line newsletters and magazines, and other information and advocacy services use mailing lists. Many of these lists now send HTML-based messages, so if you subscribe to such a list make sure that your e-mail account can read HTML-formatted text.

Discussion groups. A slightly different version of the mailing list is the discussion group. The main difference is access—discussion groups are most commonly accessed through a Web page. Yahoo!, AOL, and MSN all host their own discussion groups on-line. These are available via a Web-based interface, which you access like any other Web page—or the messages can be emailed to you if you prefer.

With mailing lists, a single person or central authority produces documents for distribution to subscribers on a fairly regular basis. Discussion groups are more like a giant bull session. Anyone can contribute a message, which is then forwarded to all subscribers.

Any group of people with a common interest can form a discussion group. Groups have been formed to discuss new software programs, research interests, or simply hobbies or political issues. Many listserver discussion groups are associated with academic organizations, associations, and societies.

Some discussion groups forward all correspondence; some are moderated by an individual to assure the relevancy of the discussion;

some incorporate messages into a period newsletter. Some groups are open; some have membership restrictions (via password).

Two warnings are in order: First, you must carefully distinguish between the address of the server that administers the distribution of messages (usually in the form listserv@address) and the address of the discussion group to which you send contributions (usually in the form groupname@address).

Second, provocative news items can trigger a deluge of comments from an ever-increasing membership. Since each subscriber receives all correspondence, hundreds of letters may suddenly appear in your mailbox.

Newsgroups. Mailing list and discussion group messages are usually e-mailed to individual subscribers. With newsgroups, e-mail messages are posted on a variety of independent networks for anyone to read and respond. Primary among these networks is Usenet (User's network), a large portion of which is carried by the Internet.

Usenet newsgroups provide a forum through which people can gossip, debate, and discuss shared interests, a conferencing system by which people from all walks of life can inform, argue with, query, and harangue each other. Newsgroups are often used to distribute the latest versions of FAQs relating to popular software or any other interest area.

Seven main categories of newsgroup postings are distributed worldwide: news, soc, talk, misc, sci, comp and rec. There is also an alt category, a miscellaneous heading for anything that does not fit elsewhere, and biz for business-related groups. In addition, there are subcategories that are limited to a specific institution or geographic area (such as UK for the United Kingdom), as well as specialized newsgroup feeds. New users should consult the FAQ posted in news.announce.newusers or visit *http://www.smr-usenet.com/*, which is an excellent source of information about Usenet.

Using newsgroups. Each newsgroup contains collections of postings or articles that are essentially e-mail messages. Postings on the same topic are assembled into threads.

A special newsreader program is required to read and respond to the postings. Such a reader (the program, that is) typically allows users to subscribe to a specific set of groups from a list of thousands available on any single network. Other newsgroups can still be retrieved, but the system does not have to load all of the messages when starting.

Newsreaders indicate the number of new articles available in each subscribed group. You can save or print a file, search for a particular term, mark files as read, go to the next article in a thread of responses, or respond directly to the author of an article with a new posting.

The other requirement for Usenet is access to a news server. Many Universities have their own news server—the Usenet server at Michigan State University, for example, is news.msu.edu. If your University does not have its own Usenet server, there are many free news servers available. A quick search using the terms "free" and "Usenet" will bring up several sites offering free Usenet access.

Finding newsgroups. When you use a newsreader to access Usenet, you will be able to search for newsgroups in which you are interested. The search program Google (*http://groups.google.com*) allows you to search and post to newsgroups. For example, searching Xnews for the term "law," results in several different newsgroups, including alt.law-enforcement, alt.tv.law-and-order, and japan.soc.law.accepted-theory. Obviously, there are many Usenet groups from which to choose.

Social considerations. Usenet groups are at once the essence and the bane of the Internet. Of all sites on the Internet, newsgroups are the preferred venue for uninhibited surfing and lurking (technical terms for scanning and reading without responding). The level of discussion can vary from the intellectual to the puerile, from mainstream to radical. While some newsgroups are moderated for content, discussion is generally uncensored, encouraging a range of belief and expression with which many are uncomfortable. As the forum for the freest expression on the Internet, newsgroups are often subject to restrictions or outright censorship.

Since the anonymity of Internet communication can give rise to relatively antisocial behavior, guides to Internet etiquette ("Netiquette") outline traditions of acceptable behavior, such as posting a message to only one newsgroup at a time (i.e., not "cross-posting"). Chug Von Rospach's "A Primer on How to Work with the Usenet Community," a guide to using Usenet politely and efficiently, is available at news.newusers.questions. Arlene Rinaldi's "The Net: User Guidelines and Netiquette" is available at *http://www.fau.edu/netiquette*.

Chat programs. One other Internet communication program does not rely on e-mail, but is somewhat similar in its effect. Chat programs allow two people to "talk" by typing remarks back and forth in real time. They offer text-based on-line communication. They work somewhat like citizens band radio. Participants an often choose from a list of available chat groups. They can enter or exit a discussion at will, identified only by a handle or nickname they have selected.

Several programs are available to users wishing to engage in on-line chat. The largest providers of chat services include IRC (Internet Relay Chat, *http://www.irchelp.org*) and ICQ ("I Seek You": *http://www.icq.com*). Both systems have their own unique software programs—ICQ software is available on the ICQ Web site, and mIRC (*http://www.mirc.com*) is the most popular of the IRC programs.

The major ISPs provide chat capabilities with their software, and both AOL and MSN offer chat options to non-subscribers. Yahoo! also has a messenger system that allows real-time chat for individuals registered on their Web page.

Voice chat is also available on-line from many chat providers. While the quality of this type of chat may not be as clear as the telephone (yet), it is a frequently used method of on-line communication.

Social Considerations

Communication using a text-based medium (whether e-mail, discussion groups, mailing lists, or Usenet) is fast and easy, but there are some language conventions of which new users should be aware. Ever resourceful, users of text-based communication both speed their task and qualify their remarks with acronyms such as BTW (by the way), IMHO (in my humble opinion), FWIW (for what it's worth), and OTOH (on the other hand). Words are stressed by using ALL CAPS or _underscoring_.

Ever playful, users have also developed a series of symbols (emoticons) to replace voice inflection and facial expressions in their letters. The best known of these symbols is the smiley, a keyboard-written image indicating delight with an idea: :^)

Finally, users of the Internet constitute their own subculture, one that has definite standards of fair play and respect for others (netiquette). One should neither YELL BY WRITING EVERYTHING IN CAPITAL LETTERS nor forward mail to large groups of people (spamming).

Since e-mail messages tend to be shorter than most other correspondence, you must take care not to be vague, ambiguous, or suggestive. Use sarcasm and humor cautiously to avoid misunderstandings.

Finally, sending e-mail or posting to groups in the privacy of your room, you might think your remarks are truly private. This is hardly the case. System administrators or your Internet provider can read e-mail. Mail you send to one person may be forwarded intact—or edited—to others without your knowledge or permission. Even if you use an anonymous "handle," your contributions to email lists and Usenet may be tracked back to you. Finally, if you leave yourself logged on to a publicly shared computer, any random person may steal your identity and spam or malign others over e-mail. This could leave you open to a warning from the computer center (at best), or legal action (at worst). Our basic message is this—take care when using on-line communication.

Telnet: The Internet as Remote Control

You can extend the cables of your computer via telephone lines to access the files of a remote computer. The keyboard and screen are your own, but you are "using" another computer.

Remote control of another computer is hardly new with the Internet. You run another computer when you dial up a bulletin board or participate on an office network. What is different with the Internet is the number of activities, and the physical range, available to you.

Many library catalogs, community bulletin boards, and academic and governmental information sites are accessible via telnet. Many colleges and universities use telnet for computerized enrollment (although many are in the process of switching to web-based services).

Most of the activities of the Internet can be accomplished by telnet-ing to public access sites.

FTP: The Internet as File Cabinet

You may never need the use of an FTP client, but this protocol is frequently used to upload and/or download files from personal computers to Web servers. Chances are good that you have probably used an FTP client without even knowing it.

For example, if you decide to create your own Web page using a free service, you may want to upload a photo of yourself for the main page. The only way to do this is to prepare the file on your own computer, then use FTP to upload that file. Most likely, the Web service will have a handy application for you to use.

Summary

This chapter has outlined the major features of the Internet and how to access them. Of course, the only way to really learn about the Internet is to log in and start surfing.

Getting Help

Computer education has always been a social affair. When in need of help, users as friends of colleagues who are, generally, only one step ahead in their computer expertise.

For most students, help is as close as their computing center. Many computing centers provide handouts and offer mini-courses. Guides to the use of services and software are often posted on university networks.

On-line guides. An extensive menu of guides to all aspects of the Internet and its resources is maintained by John December (*http://www.december.com/net/tools*).

Frequently Asked Questions (FAQs). Responses to frequently asked questions are available as FAQ files. There are FAQs for almost all aspects of Internet content and use:

- alt.fan.monty-python FAQ
- Anonymous FTP Frequently Asked Questions (FAQ) List
- Economist's Resources on the Internet
- FAQ: How to find people's e-mail addresses
- How to Read Chinese Text on Usenet: FAQ for alt.Chinese.txt.

Copies of FAQs are generally available from the relevant Web site or Usenet newsgroup. Usenet FAQs are posted on the newsgroups news.announce.newusers, news.answers, or news.newusers.questions.

FAQs have become standard information on most Web sites. For example, the Central Intelligence Agency has a FAQ located at: *http://www.cia.gov/cia/public_affairs/faq.html.*

Chapter 2

Internet Applications for Criminal Justice

Now that you are familiar with the basics of Internet lingo and applications, we move on to discuss what the Internet offers to students of criminal justice. This chapter discusses the use of "official" web sites for newspapers, television and radio as well as important sources of information created to dispense criminal justice information.

Current Events

Much of your discussions in criminal justice courses likely focus on current events. We are constantly searching for new solutions to the crime problem, there are always high profile cases being tried somewhere in the world, and the problem of terrorism is frequently in the news.

Your professors are sure to be impressed if you attend your courses with a solid knowledge of current events in the field. Many of the sources you would use to keep abreast of current events IRL (in real life) are probably the same sources you would use to keep track of happenings on-line: radio, newspapers and television.

Newspapers

All large city newspapers have Web sites that contain updated information. In fact, the advantage of having a news site on-line is the ability to constantly update information. On September 11, 2001, many of the large news sites were inundated with users trying to find the most recent information on the tragedy as it unfolded. Many sites were unable to handle the large volume of users, and they were inaccessible for some time.

You might be surprised how similar a newspaper's Web site appears to the actual printed version of the newspaper. For example, the front page of NewYorkTimes.com appears as:

College newspapers also are beginning to develop their own Web sites. You can examine The Daily Californian from UC Berkeley (*http://www.dailycal.org*) and the University of Texas' Daily Texan (*http://www.dailytexanonline.com*) without ever leaving your dorm room.

What makes the Internet an especially good source of international news is the wide availability of foreign newspapers with English language Web sites. You can read about crime in Japan in the Japan Times On-line (*http://www.japantimes.co.jp*) or keep up-to-date with events in England in The Times (*http://www.thetimes.co.uk*).

The following American newspaper sites are very popular among Internet users:

- The New York Times *http://www.nytimes.com/*
- The Chicago Tribune *http://www.Chicago.tribune.com/*
- The Washington Post *http://www.washingtonpost.com/*
- The Los Angeles Times *http://www.latimes.com/*

Television

The large cable networks that feature information on the news have Web sites that are very similar to newspaper sites. CNN (*http://www.cnn.com/*), MSNBC (*http://www.msnbc.com/*) and Fox News (*http://www.foxnews.com/*) all run detailed Web sites.

Since these sites typically group stories by topic, there is usually a special section for information on crime. The CNN Web page includes a "Law" section, while MSNBC has a "Crime and Punishment" area. These are both excellent resources for current information.

Internet Radio

Yes, even radio stations are increasingly available on-line. Some radio stations have their own Web sites, such as National Public Radio (*http://www.npr.org/*), but other Internet sites are available that list thousands of local radio stations also accessible via the Internet (*http://www.live-radio.net/* is but one of such sites). Feeling homesick? Find your favorite local radio station from home on your computer, and forget about studying for a little while (but not for too long!).

Finding Paper Topics

A constant source of anxiety for students is coming up with suitable topics for college papers. Indeed, the choice of topic will greatly affect your grade on papers. You can set your work apart from other students by using the Internet to develop interesting ideas for papers. A professor who's teaching a course on Community Policing will probably get a stack of papers entitled "Community Policing" (as you can guess, reading 40 papers on the same topic is not very exciting). You can make your paper stand out by selecting a more current and topical issue, perhaps "International Terrorism and its Effect on Community Policing in the United States."

My idea for this hypothetical paper above was the result of a search of the MSNBC Web page for the term "community policing". I discovered an article discussing the fact that funding for programs combating international terrorism will result in budget cuts to the "COPS" program, which provides funding to local communities for community policing. Thus, a paper topic is born.

Searching news sites is a good way to find paper ideas that are current and interesting. While you may be inclined to search the Internet generally, this is less likely to reveal current issues on criminal justice topics. You will probably find some good sources for your paper — searching Yahoo! for "community policing" will lead you to the COPS office (*http://www.usdoj.gov/cops/*), The Police Foundation (*http://www.policefoundation.org/*) and the National Center for Community Policing (*http://cj.msu.edu/~people/cp/*) just to name a few. These are all excellent sources for general information about community policing.

Sources of Academic Information

Finding information from news sources is fine for some applications, but chances are good that you'll also want to be familiar with the academic literature on a topic. Stories in the media are sometimes written from the perspective of one person or a small group of people. You should always strengthen your argument with findings from empirical research.

For example, while reading an on-line news source you discover that your home state is in the process of passing legislation that will allow 13-year-old juveniles to be tried as adults. The news story contains several quotes from lawmakers who favor the law, and several interviews with community members who believe the new law will reduce juvenile crime.

This is interesting information, but you might wonder what such a law is actually meant to accomplish, and whether other states that have passed such laws have found them effective. The place to look for this type of information is in the academic literature—books and journal articles.

Academic books are (of course) available in your college library and not usually available on-line—although excerpts of books can frequently be found on web sites that sell books, such as *http://www.amazon.com* or *http://www.barnesandnoble.com*. You'll have an easier time finding journal articles on-line, which is usually better anyway. Journal articles typically contain the most recent research on criminal justice topics. Because of the length of time it takes to write and publish books, some are outdated by the time they hit the shelves!

How you access journal articles will depend on your individual college library. For instance, here are some possible locations for journals in your library:

- New journals are typically kept in the "Current Publications" section of the library
- Older journals may be hardbound and kept in the stacks with the books.
- If your library subscribes to an on-line article service (such as ProQuest or Wilson FirstSearch), you may be able to access the articles on-line. Check with your library information desk or the library web page for more information.
- Some journals offer on-line access to institutions that subscribe to the print version.
- Finally, some journals are published solely using electronic format (such as the Journal of Criminal Justice and Popular culture at *http://www.albany.edu/scj/jcjpc/*). They may be free to view, or you may have to pay a subscription to access their pages.

Web Sites for Criminal Justice

   In the process of surfing the 'net, you will no doubt encounter many web sites dedicated to criminal justice. These sites are sometimes created by criminal justice agencies and organizations, and sometimes created by individuals with an interest in criminal justice (be sure to read the section entitled "Verifying Sources" in Chapter Three before putting too much faith in random Web sites).

Theories of crime. There are some good resources on-line to learn about criminological theory. For example, *http://www.crimetheory.com* is maintained by a professor at the University of Washington, and contains several resources for learning, researching, and teaching about theories of crime. Other pages focus on specific theories of crime, or particular perspectives. You will find some outstanding sources of information on critical criminology at *http://www.critcrim.org*.

Professional organizations. The American Society of Criminology (*http://www.asc41.com*) and the Academy of Criminal Justice Sciences both maintain home pages with important links to criminal justice information, including professional positions (see Chapter Four on "Finding a Career" for more information).

Official government sites. You can also use the Web sites of professional organizations to find important information about the study of crime cross-culturally. For example, the Australian Institute of Criminology contains a wealth of information about crime "down under" (*http://www.aic.gov.au/*), and you might use that information for a comparative study of crime between Australia and the United States. To provide access to as many people as possible, many international Web sites have English-language versions in addition to their main page. The Korean Institute of Criminology is an excellent example of this, with their main page in Korean (*http://www.kic.re.kr*), and an additional page in English (*http://www.kic.re.kr/engl/e_main.php*). You might also be interested in the Scandinavian Research Council for Criminology at *http://www.nsfk.org*.

Research institutes. There are many private research institutes that study crime and publish their findings. The two most well known are the Vera Institute of Justice (*http://www.vera.org*) and the RAND Corporation (*http://www.rand.org/crim/*). There are a large number of smaller, nonprofit research institutes that maintain a presence on the Web, such as the Institute for Law and Justice (*http://www.ilj.org/*).

Interest groups. There are an increasing number of Web sites that focus on a particular issue, or have a vested interest (or just a strong attitude) about some aspect of the criminal justice system. These exist on every aspect of the criminal justice system—police (especially use of excessive force or police pursuit), courts, and corrections. The American Civil Liberties Union, for example, maintains a criminal justice Web page detailing abuses of the system and information on civil liberties (*http://www.aclu.org/issues/criminal/hmcj.html*). The Center for Rational Correctional Policy (*http://www.correctionalpolicy.com/*) argues against the retributive sentencing system, and Families Against Mandatory Minimums (*http://www.famm.org*) lobbies for the removal of mandatory sentences for drug and weapon offenses.

The important thing to remember about these kinds of sites is that they are not objective researchers presenting findings from research. While they should present the findings from unbiased research, they may only present information relevant to their cause and omit anything that does not support it. Thus, you should judge the value of the information they present very carefully. Just like any debate on an important topic, you should attempt to research all sides of a position before making up your mind.

Finally, school projects often make for very interesting Web sites. You can learn about criminal sentencing procedure at the "Anatomy of a Murder" page (*http://library.thinkquest.org/2760/homep.htm*), which was created by high school students.

Summary

Hopefully, this section has enlightened you as to the resources available for criminal justice students on the Internet. Many of the links above were found on *http://www.yahoo.com* in the "Criminal Justice" (Home> Government> Law> Criminal Justice) and "Criminology" (Home> Social Science> Sociology> Criminology) categories. I strongly recommend using search engines to find even more sites discussing interesting criminal justice topics.

Simply typing the words "death penalty" into Yahoo! or Google will bring forth sites discussing both sides of issue. Don't just dip your toes in the water—take a deep breath and dive in!

Exercises

1. Visit the College News list of college newspapers at *http://www.collegenews.com/campusnews.htm*. Is your college newspaper listed? Select a newspaper and find some information on campus crime (try looking for "Police Blotter" or "Police Briefs"). What kinds of crime have occurred recently on that campus? If you were to design a study of crime on your college campus, how might the college's Internet sources help you find data?

2. Trying to define what constitutes a crime can vary depending on whom you ask. For example, the concept of corporate crime can be defined in different ways. Some refer to corporate crime as any crime committed in the workplace, while others use this term to refer to crimes such as embezzlement and fraud by those in positions of power in organizations. Use the Internet to find out how different people define behavior known as "corporate crime".

3. One current issue of concern to the public today is the increasing use of handguns in the commission of crime. Using a search engine, find at least two opposing viewpoints on the relationship between guns and crime. How do these different viewpoints explain their position regarding gun control and crime? Do they propose any solutions for elevated rates of gun-related deaths in the United States?

4. Many people believe that politics has a large influence over which crimes the public believes are serious. Can you find evidence that some

crimes are more "popular" at certain times than others? (When searching, try to pay attention to the dates when items appeared on the Internet).

> *Tips for Searching*
> Try to find sites that focus on an issue such as gun crime or corporate crime. Before searching, can you identify specific organizations that may have an opinion on these topics? Try to find their home pages for their stance on these issues.

5. One of the tasks of researchers in criminal justice is to explain criminal behavior using a combination of sociological, psychological, and biological theories. Using a search engine, try to find examples of how biological differences in individuals can be used to explain variations in criminal behavior.

6. How many resources can you find on the Internet in your home state for victims of crime? Are these related to specific types of crime, such as rape or domestic violence, or are they more general? If you have trouble finding resources, try looking up the home pages of victim's rights groups.

7. Community policing has been hailed as a means of controlling crime through problem-solving and community-based law enforcement. How is community policing being implemented across the country? Can you find Internet sites that deal with training community police officers? How does this differ from traditional training techniques?

8. What is the difference between the type of work done by the FBI and work done by the ATF? Access each agency's home page to determine the differences between them.

9. There has been much debate about hiring qualifications for male and female police officers. Some believe that female officers should have less stringent physical requirements than male officers, while others believe both sexes should have to endure the same requirements for hiring. Can you find any information on the Internet that discusses this issue? Are

there Web pages for local law enforcement agencies that publish their hiring requirements? If so, are they different for men and women?

10. The Supreme Court is the last court of appeals for inmates on death row. The Court has heard numerous arguments that the death penalty is unconstitutional and should be deemed cruel and unusual punishment. Find a Web page that contains Supreme Court decisions. What kinds of cases has the Supreme Court heard on the death penalty in the last five years? What are the main issues under which death row inmates have appealed?

11. Using a search engine, search for the term "habeas corpus". How is this term defined on Web sites? Has any recent legislation attempted to restrict the use of habeas corpus appeals?

12. In some states, a grand jury is used to indict an individual suspected of committing a crime. Recently, the system of using a grand jury has come under fire as being wasteful of time and money. Many believe the prosecuting attorney should have the power to indict cases without the use of a grand jury (and in some states, this is possible). Find a number of opinions on this issue on the Internet. Do people who support the grand jury system have anything in common (that is, can they all be classified under a specific political affiliation or belief)? What about those who oppose the current grand jury system in the United States?

13. Concerned by seemingly unlimited power of judges at sentencing, some states have created sentencing commissions to write guidelines for punishing offenders. How many states currently have sentencing guidelines in use? Read about the Federal Sentencing Guidelines at the home page of the United States Sentencing Commission (*http://www.mpp.org/ussc/theussc.html*). This will help you find terms for which to search.

14. One of the purposes of punishment in the United States is to keep people from committing more crimes. This is known as deterrence, and it is meant to reduce recidivism rates following punishment. Find an

opinion on the Internet regarding harsh punishment deterring offenders from future crime.

15. Some people feel that incarcerating juvenile offenders does more harm than good. Specifically, they believe it is better to divert juvenile offenders from the criminal justice system so they are not affected adversely by the realities of the system. How many different juvenile diversion programs can you find on the Internet? What do these offenders do in place of being incarcerated?

16. The correctional system in the United States has grown tremendously since prison reform began following the American Revolution. Today, private companies have begun to take over the job of managing prisons, jails, and community corrections. Can you find a site on the Internet for one of these private companies? Based on their description, do you think they would do an adequate job of running a prison, or should that be left to the government?

Tips for Searching
It may be easiest to find information about private corrections companies using an organized search mechanism, such as Yahoo (*http://www.yahoo.com/*), which organizes sites by categories.

17. There is an obvious link between social class (or socioeconomic status) and criminal behavior. Using a search engine, search for the terms "poverty" and "crime" occurring in the same record. What kinds of explanations do authors give for this relationship?

Chapter 3
Using the Internet for Criminal Justice Research

The previous chapter discussed how to find information on criminal justice issues on-line; however, the Internet can also be used to *create* new research. Thousands of statistics and data sources are available on-line for students to download and analyze. Because crime data are frequently available to the public, you can easily access data sources and include relevant statistics in research papers and reports.

Internet Concerns

The resources of the Internet are indeed enormous and ever expanding. Resources unheard of only a few years ago are now commonplace. But, as we suggested, you must first have some idea of what's out there, and know how to find what you want when you want it.

Know Your Options

Knowing where to look depends greatly on knowing where you might look. You should be aware of the existence of, and uses of, a number of electronic resources—both in general and in criminal justice, such as:

- Databases (both public and commercial)
- Abstract services
- Specialized on-line library connections
- Professional Associations
- State and government agencies
- Nonprofit organizations
- Usenet newsgroups and listserver discussion groups
- Anonymous FTP software archives.

Know How to Get What You Want

Knowing what is on the Internet, and where it is, is only half the story. You also have to know how to get where you want to go. You must understand the variety of services and the programs necessary to access those services.

To use the services effectively, you should understand how each service organizes and accesses information. That means such things as knowing the addresses of relevant web sites and why you might use one search engine over another.

To use the Internet—and your own time—effectively, you must distinguish between active discovery and idle diversion, between productive research and sheer busywork.

Authorship, Authenticity, Authoritativeness, and Value

When you pick up a book or newspaper, you have a certain confidence in the authenticity of the material. Examining a book or professional journal in a library, you are aware that it has been selected from among competing texts and reviewed by an editor prior to publication, and selected from among competing publications by a librarian for inclusion in the collection. The title and copyright page attest to the true author and place and date of publication. And you are reasonably certain the document exists in the form intended by the author.

With the Internet, all of these assumptions may fall under suspicion. When it is easy to create personae, it is hard to verify credentials. Internet citations have no page numbers of publication dates, and a reader pursuing a citation may find the text has been moved or altered—with no way to know the difference.

Any source found on the Internet must be judged as to its value and authenticity. These days, anyone can create a web page—your task as a consumer of information is to weigh every source carefully. For example, if you find an article discussing the current statistics on handgun ownership on the web page of the Bureau of Alcohol, Tobacco and Firearms *(http://www.atf.treas.gov/)* you'll probably think that information is correct. However, if you find different statistics on "Bob's Gun Page", you might question those statistics. Who's Bob? Why does he have a web page about guns? What are his sources? You get the idea—the source of each piece of information should be carefully evaluated before you base your research on it.

On the whole, Internet data is no more authoritative than any other—and in many cases less so. While we may delight in the fact that we can post anything we want on the Internet, when we are looking for information we would like to be able to distinguish beforehand between a professor's treatise and Johnny's seventh grade school report. "Anyone who has attempted to obtain information from the Internet," an editorial in the Journal of Chemical Education observed, " knows that you are as likely to find garbage as you are to find quality information." The affiliation of a server may suggest a certain degree of reliability, but that in itself should indicate neither approval nor review by anyone else at that institution.

While the Internet may have the richness and range of a world-class encyclopedia, that does not mean you want to (or need to) read every article. Much of the current material on the Internet is out-dated or only offers snippets of information. Much of the discussion on newsgroups is simply chatter. Just because you can download thousands of files does not mean you need any of them.

On the bright side, since it is easier to publish material on the Internet than it is to publish books, information available on the Internet is often more up-to-date than information in printed texts. But that is useful only for information that changes frequently, or has changed recently.

Internet Tactics and Strategies

Is the Internet the Best Tool to Use?

You may turn to the Internet to save time, to save effort, or to find better sources of information. But just because you have access to the Internet does not mean the Internet is necessarily the best tool for a particular project. Many times, other procedures are quicker, easier, and more certain to yield results.

Try the Obvious First

The general rule should be: Try the obvious first. This seems self evident, but it often needs restating. To find the Latin name for "lions" you can turn on your computer, logon to your Internet service, access a search program, input a search term, wait for a response, evaluate the sources provided, and continue onto a specific location. Or you can flip open a collegiate dictionary and look it up. There's a lesson there.

Networking for Knowledge

The car manufacturer Packard long ago had a slogan: Ask the man who owns one. With research: ask someone who knows. You can use e-mail to communicate with others, or check archives of frequently asked questions of a relevant newsgroup. You can participate in the communication of a discussion group.

Overall, however, you are more likely to gain fresh insights and understanding through the interchange of talking to someone else than you are punching keys on a keyboard and staring at a computer screen.

What You Can, and Cannot, Find

The Internet was developed for scientists to exchange data and ideas. While much of the emphasis has shifted to commercial and entertainment applications, the Internet remains a vital link in academic and scientific communication.

In recent years governmental agencies at all levels have made increasing amounts of information available on the Internet. Many professional associations and interest groups maintain home pages on the World Wide Web.

Still, no one gives anything of value away for free. While you can access some encyclopedias on the Internet, the premier volume, Encyclopedia Britannica, is available only by commercial subscription.

Full texts of professional journals, are, for the most part, available only to subscribers. Nevertheless, journals increasingly offer tables of contents, archives or abstracts, and supplemental tables, illustrations, or data, as well as searchable indices of past issues on the Internet.

Commercial full-text databases such as Lexis-Nexis can often be accessed via the Internet for a fee. Students and faculty, however, may have access to such proprietary databases on-line or on CD-ROM in college libraries.

Budgeting Your Time and On-line Time

The general rule for efficient use of the Internet is simple: log on, get what you want, and log off. You want to know what you're looking for beforehand and have a plan for accessing it. You want to get the information you seek, and get out. This is especially true when you are incurring hourly expenses imposed by on-line services and Internet providers.

You can save time and money by downloading information for later perusal. Off-line time is chapter than on-line time, and hard copies are easier to read than text on screens.

Both text and graphical interface programs offer some means of automatically capturing on-screen text during a session. You can save hypertext pages on the World Wide Web in a cache directory for closer examination off-line.

Spend your time on-line evaluating information, not looking up addresses. Keep a list of frequently used web sites in your "Favorites" folder or save them as bookmarks. In your career as a college student, you will find yourself returning to those frequently used sites repeatedly.

Citations and Plagiarism

You can save time and effort by downloading documents instead of finding published texts and photocopying them. You can then insert that text directly into your own writing.

While a great convenience, this process has obvious dangers. You can confuse your text with text that you have downloaded, and in so doing commit the crime of plagiarism. And you can lose track of information for proper citations.

To avoid plagiarism, store downloaded text with a special font— such as *italic* or SMALL CAPITAL LETTERS—and change the font only when the material has been property cited within your discussion.

The address of Internet documents is often equivalent to the publication data associated with books. The method in which this material is cited in the reference section of your paper will depend on the style you are using, but you can find many sources of information on this topic on-line. There are also some very good style guidebooks such as the Chicago Manual of Style or the Publication Manual of the American Psychological Association, whose most recent versions include citation of on-line sources.

Resources for Internet Research

There are essentially two approaches to research on the Internet: browsing and searching. Searching begins with selecting a search program or search engine and a search term or terms. Browsing requires, once again, a choice of where to start browsing.

Browsing

A good start point for browsing is a search engine that groups web sites by topical areas. For example, if you are interested in earning a Master's degree in criminal justice, a list of programs offering graduate programs is a good place to start. If you tried to find graduate programs in CJ by using a keyword search, you would likely end up with a very large number of sites—many of which would not even be relevant to your needs. Instead, a site that groups web sites into categories is a much better solution. Yahoo! (*http://www.yahoo.com*) is a good example of a hierarchical search engine.

Searching

There may be times when a keyword search is more appropriate for your needs. Do you have to find a web site that discusses the process of waiving juveniles to adult court? Since that topic does not fit neatly into one category, we might try to search for the keywords "waiver" and "juvenile" to see if we get any hits.

Search engines that are hierarchical (i.e., grouped by category) are also keyword search engines. There are too many search engines available to list them all--Yahoo! lists 114 "all-in-one search engines" alone. When you include other types that number increases exponentially. The major engines include Google (*http://www.google.com*), Iwon (*http://www.iwon.com*), and Excite (*http://www.excite.com*). As you become more comfortable with the Internet, you will no doubt find one that you are most comfortable with and use it frequently.

Downloadable Data

The amount of criminal justice data available on-line is truly extraordinary. Even some interest groups have their own data available for download (as with any source, it is vital to assess the reliability of such data before using it). To illustrate some of what is available for students, we briefly discuss three major sources of criminal justice data: The Sourcebook of Criminal Justice Statistics, The Uniform Crime Reports and The National Archive of Criminal Justice Data.

The Sourcebook of Criminal Justice Statistics

Maintained by the School of Criminal Justice at the State University of New York at Albany, the Sourcebook is an easy-to-use source of criminal justice data (*http://www.albany.edu/sourcebook*). Statistics are organized by topic, and are available for multiple years.

As an illustration, one of the many topics available focuses on public attitudes on police use of force. As seen below, these data are available from 1973-2000.

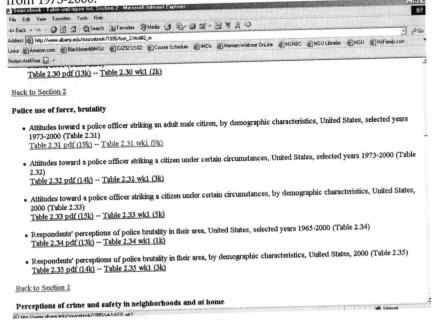

You will notice that there are two options available for accessing these data. One is called a "pdf" file, and is a graphic image that must be viewed using Adobe Acrobat (you can find a free Acrobat reader at *http://www.adobe.com*). The other file is a "wk1" file, which is a type of spreadsheet file. This file extension indicates that you can download the data into a spreadsheet program, such as Lotus or Excel. The benefit of downloading the data directly to your computer means that you can use a statistical program (such as SPSS or SAS) to analyze the data yourself.

For the moment, let's look at the data in the "pdf" file. When you open this file, you will see the following statistics:

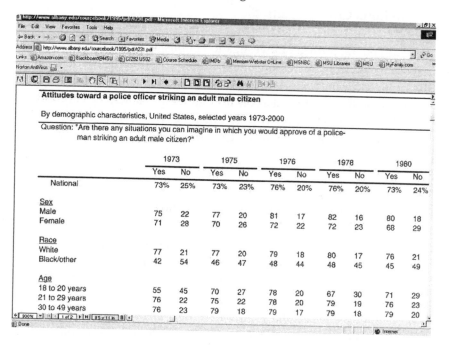

Notice that male respondents are more likely to support police use of force than female respondents (75% versus 71% in 1973). Also, support for police use of force increased from 1973 to 1978—75% of male respondents support use of force in 1973, but by 1978 this percentage was up to 82%.

In years past, the information contained in the Sourcebook was distributed by mail to researchers. Each yearly volume was the size of a large telephone book, and many researchers (myself included) had an entire shelf filled with volumes of the Sourcebook.

With the advent of the Internet, the Sourcebook no longer needed to be mailed to subscribers. Now it is easily accessible, and searching for the relevant crime statistics is even easier than the old paper version. In addition, the monetary savings are extraordinary—imagine the cost of mailing several thousand telephone books to criminal justice researchers! Today, the same can be accomplished by sending a single email to a subscriber list notifying them of a new version.

The Uniform Crime Reports

The Federal Bureau of Investigation publishes crime statistics using data collected from law enforcement agencies around the country. Called the Uniform Crime Reports (*http://www.fbi.gov/ucr/ucr.htm*), these statistics can be used to make conclusions about crime trends around the country—in fact, whenever you read that the crime rate is increasing, news agencies are probably using UCR data provided to them by the FBI.

The National Archive of Criminal Justice Data

Perhaps the easiest way to find data on-line is through a data repository, such as the National Archive of Criminal Justice Data available through the Interuniversity Consortium of Political and Social Research at the University of Michigan (*http://www.icpsr.umich.edu/NACJD/*). At the time of this writing, the NACJD contained over 385 data sets available to students at colleges and Universities who are members of the Consortium.

The data files available in the NACJD represent the most current and comprehensive criminal justice data available to researchers. Each data file in the archive is unformatted, with syntax available to read files into SPSS (the Statistical Program for the Social Sciences) or SAS.

Creating Your Own Data Source

Most undergraduate students in criminal justice will be able to find data sources easily available for research papers. However, some of you may take on more detailed research projects, such as an honor's thesis, in which you create and analyze your own data. While this may sound like an enormous task, it doesn't have to be. You can create a unique research project with some basic research skills and the Internet.

Using Existing Web Sources

Yet another benefit of the Internet is the amount of publicly available data. Creating a data source is simply a matter of collecting information and entering it into a computer program for data analysis (such as SPSS or SAS).

Let's say you're interested in creating a database of death penalty legislation for each state. You'll probably want to include variables such as:

- Does the state have the death penalty?
- What is the method of execution for each death penalty state?
- How many people are currently on death row in each state?
- How many women and people of color are currently on death row?

Some of this information may already exist in one form or another. You should probably begin by visiting a death penalty site, such as The Death Penalty Information Center (*http://www.deathpenaltyinfo.org/*). If that site does not contain all the information you need, you may decide to visit the web pages for individual states. Texas, for example, has a comprehensive page dedicated to their Death Row (*http://www.tdcj.state.tx.us/stat/deathrow.htm*). Finally, news sites may also be helpful in tracking down statistics and information about offenders.

Content Analysis

Content analysis involves creating a data source from media sources. Our purpose here is to provide you with an overview of this technique, so if you are truly interested in this topic we recommend you find a book detailing the specifics of content analysis.

One common use of content analysis involves measuring violence on television. Researchers may systematically watch television every evening during the "family hour" and count how many instances of violence they witness.

A similar type of study can be extended to the Internet. Parents today are concerned that their children are exposed to sexually explicit material on-line. While many of these sites are unavailable to minors, there are of course exceptions to the rule. In some cases, pornographic sites purposefully include key words on their sites that they know are common search terms. These particular sites may be found my children. To measure this, we might want to run a search for commonplace keywords and count the number of sites returned that contain sexually explicit materials.

Newspapers and books are commonly used for content analysis, and with electronic versions of both available on-line, the task of sorting through documents has become considerably easier. You may want to conduct a study of media accounts of terrorism. A study of international newspaper articles might allow you to compare how different countries view the seriousness of terrorism around the world.

Summary

There are numerous opportunities for criminal justice research on the Internet. We cannot stress enough that extreme care must be taken when determining the validity of on-line sources. Remember that anyone can make a web page stating anything. Try to corroborate all sources.

In addition to literature sources, data sources are also widely available on-line. Many of these are downloadable directly into statistical software packages that can be used in papers and reports.

Supplementing your papers with statistical support will strengthen your arguments, and hopefully result in a high grade!

Exercises

1. You have been asked to create a database containing information about all terrorist incidents that have occurred worldwide in the last five years. How might you go about compiling this information? Can you find a web site that summarizes these incidents?

2. Access the Bureau of Justice Statistics home page at *http://www.ojp.usdoj.gov/bjs/welcome.html*. Based on reports presented here that use national level statistics, would you say that crime is rising or falling in the United States?

3. You are assigned a paper on gang violence in your juvenile justice course, and decide to look through The New York Times to find stories about youth gangs in New York. Using their web page (*http://www.newyorktimes.com*), search for occurrences of the term "gang violence" in their archives. How many of these articles are editorials? How do these authors describe gang members? Are the articles taking a neutral viewpoint, or are they more opinionated?

4. Access the National Archive of Criminal Justice Data at the Inter-university Consortium for Political and Social Research (*http://www.icpsr.umich.edu/NACJD/*). Try to find a data set that deals with expenditures for police departments, and read the abstract that describes the data. Where were the data originally collected? Do the authors present any findings from analyzing these data?

5. How many instances of police excessive force were reported in the past six months in the United States? Rather than using a search engine, find a news site that updates its stories daily. Make sure the site has its own search engine, and use that to find recent instances of police use of excessive force.

6. Recent statistics on individuals incarcerated in the United States are disproportionately minority citizens (this information can be found in the Bureau of Justice Statistics Corrections page at *http://www.ojp.usdoj.gov/bjs/prisons.html*). How might we explain the difference between rates of incarceration for black and white offenders? Can you find Internet sites that suggest how to solve this problem?

7. Go to the web page for the British Society of Criminology (*http://www.britsoccrim.org*). What recommendations to they make for researchers engaging in criminological research? How might these guidelines help you to conduct ethical research using data collected on the Internet?

8. There are many opinions about police use of force in the United States. Conduct a regional comparison of attitudes about use of force from editorials in regional on-line newspapers. Do the various regions of the United States (Northeast, Southeast, Midwest, Southwest, Pacific Northwest) differ in terms of their experiences with regard to police use of force?

Chapter 4
Criminal Justice Careers On-line

In addition to the academic resources described thus far, the Internet is also useful to those of you who are nearing the end of your undergraduate degree. As the light at the end of the tunnel gets brighter, the Internet can help you make sure that the light is really the "end of the line", and not an oncoming train.

Career Aids On-line

If this is your first time on the job market, you will need some assistance preparing your resume and learning how to make present yourself in the best light possible. Some students are lucky enough to have resources at their college or university, but others will have to forge ahead on their own. We suggest you take the time to use Internet resources that focus on presentation, and being able to "put your best foot forward".

Career Options

Simply because you are majoring in criminal justice does not mean you know exactly what career you would like to pursue. You may need to do some research on-line to determine your options. One excellent source of information on this topic is The Occupational Outlook Handbook (*http://www.bls.gov/oco*). Published by the Bureau of Labor Statistics, this handbook gives descriptions for many different career paths.

For example, your studies in criminal justice may have focused on juvenile delinquency. A search for the term "delinquency" in the BLS Handbook resulted in two possible career paths: social work, and education and community service. Here is a peek at the job description for social workers:

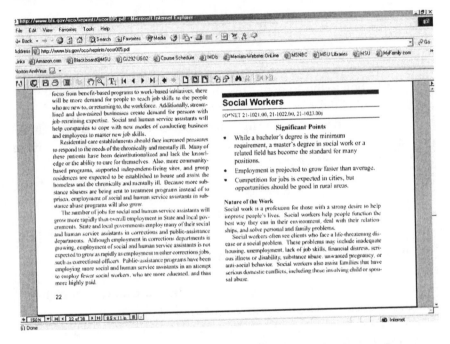

As you can see, this is extremely informative for students who are trying to decide on a career following graduation. You may even determine that the job you want requires additional education, such as an MSW (Master of Social Work).

Some sites on the Internet offer assessment testing to determine your "ideal" career. These can be fun, but probably aren't a wise investment of your time and money—most of these sites will charge you a set fee for their assessment. Just as with other Internet searches, you may find web sites that organize much of this information topically. Take a look at *http://www.careerplanning.org*, which lists links to hundreds of career planning aids.

Résumé Writing

There are many sites that can help you put together an impressive résumé. At *http://www.jobweb.com*, you can browse through the recommended essentials for an effective résumé. There are even web sites for which the sole purpose is résumé and cover letter writing (such as *http://www.resume-cover-letter.info*).

Take care to visit reputable sites during your search—one web site we found for this section required signing in to access their services, which entitled the registrant to a free copy of their credit report. Remember, don't give anyone access to your email account unless you want to receive email from them, and possibly anyone to whom they give (or sell) your name.

Interviewing

If the résumé gets your foot in the door, the interview can "make or break" the whole thing. Internet resources in this area are typically limited to sites with pointers for successful interviewing. As with career planning, some of these sites will offer their services for a price, but most good common-sense information about interviewing for jobs can be found for free. Dana Curtis at Harvard University's Office of Career Services has put together an excellent resource for interviewing *at http://www.ocs.fas.harvard.edu/html/intview.html*.

Career Opportunities and How to Find Them

There are many opportunities for students earning a criminal justice degree, ranging from law enforcement to investigation to counseling. The key to finding the right career is research, and the Internet is an excellent source of research on careers in criminal justice. Just as doing your homework helped you to earn good grades while in school, doing your homework and determining what prospective employers are looking for will help you land a good job.

Law Enforcement

Local agencies. Suppose you would very much like to be a police officer in Dallas, Texas. You could navigate directly to the Dallas Police Department web site (*http://www.dallaspolice.net*) and visit their "Recruiting" section. Visiting this page will inform you that DPD is looking for recruits with:

- At least 45 credits in college with at least a "C" average
- A minimum age of 21 (or 19 with 60 college credits)
- U.S. citizenship
- An honorable military discharge (if applicable)
- A valid driver's license
- A clean criminal record (naturally).

In addition, the DPD web page lists salaries and benefits for officers in their department. Having this information prior to application will help you decide if this is a position in which you are truly interested. Here's an example of the benefits they have to offer in the DPD:

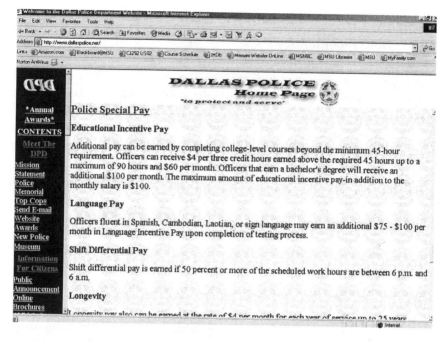

You can expand your search for law enforcement careers in the Dallas area by using an Internet search engine. A search at Google.com for the terms "Dallas" and "police" returns several sites that may help you find a position, such as:

- The University of Texas at Dallas Police Department
- The Fort Worth Police Department
- The Arlington Police Department

Browse the list of results, and you may come across web sites that list more law enforcement agencies in the area, such as the Tarrant County Sheriff's Department (*http://www.tarrantcounty.com/sheriff/site/default.asp*) and the Texas Department of Public Safety (*http://www.txdps.state.tx.us*). There are also a large number of smaller towns surrounding the Dallas area that have their own Web sites. By paying special attention to the wider variety of career opportunities, you're more likely to find a position suited to your needs.

Federal Job Opportunities

If you are interested in pursuing a federal position, there are detailed application instructions depending on the position. Many web sites will offer to "mediate" for you with the government for a fee—that is, they will sometimes send you a list of all Federal jobs available, or send you a guide to getting through the application process. Keep in mind that the government itself provides this information free of charge.

USAJOBS is a good example of how the United States government disseminates career information (*http://www.usajobs.opm.gov/*). They even offer a method of applying on-line, although this is usually just a first step. Most government positions require a background check for all applicants.

Finally, as a criminal justice major, don't limit yourself to the law enforcement agencies, such as the Federal Bureau of Investigation or the Bureau of Alcohol, Tobacco and Firearms. All government agencies hire inspectors, and many criminal justice graduates work as inspectors for agencies you might not expect (like the Department of Health and Human Services or the Department of Agriculture).

General Career Aids

Sometimes, for many reasons, students choose to look for jobs outside the area of their college degree. If this applies to you, you'll be happy to know there are many sources of job information on-line that is not limited to the criminal justice area.

Websites for job seekers are extremely prevalent, including Hot Jobs (*http://www.hotjobs.com*) and Monster (*http://www.monster.com*). In fact, both sites contain categories for "Law Enforcement and Security" positions. You may also want to search for government positions here in addition to the government web sites.

There are also Usenet groups that contain discussion about available career opportunities. Looking for a job in New York? Trying browsing through the posts to nyc.jobs.misc. You can even add your résumé to the (very long) list at nyc.jobs.wanted.

Showcase Yourself On-line

The availability to create free web pages on the Internet gives job seekers a whole new way to present themselves to prospective employers. While you might not be able to throw that paper résumé away just yet, having a copy of your résumé on-line allows potential employers to access your information 24 hours a day. In the section below, we list some of the possible ways in which you might create a web page to give you a leg up in the job search.

Résumé

Your on-line résumé will probably look the same as your "hard-copy" résumé with one exception: An HTML document can contain links to other web sites. In essence, you are providing direct contact between the company for whom you would like to work and your references.

Possible links you might use include educational institutions, web pages of previous employers (if you feel comfortable including this), and email contact information for your references.

Practical Experience

Have you completed an internship or is there a job experience you had in which you were very interested? Make sure to make a point of it on your professional web page. Use this as an opportunity to demonstrate the important skills you acquired in the position, and how those skills will translate into proficiency in the position for which you're looking.

Writing Samples

All word processors have the ability to save documents in HTML format. You can share your best work with potential employers by uploading your papers to a web page. If you're lucky enough to have a publication, you might be able to provide a link to it at the publication site.

Summary

Finding a position following can graduation can be a difficult process. Using the Internet to its maximum benefit not only helps to showcase your skills on-line, but also demonstrates that you are comfortable using the latest technology. Employers trying to fill positions are looking for people that stand out in the crowd. Set yourself apart by taking advantage of what the Internet has to offer!

Appendix A

The Instructor's Guide to Using the Internet for Criminal Justice

My first (and only) application of the Internet for my criminal justice classes was posting grades. This was a tremendous leap at the time I began this process—no longer did students have to walk across campus to my office to see their grades posted outside my door. Email also made my teaching job much easier—questions about material and grades could be answered just as easily from my home computer, and essentially extended office hours for many students.

As the Internet has developed, so have the applications for teaching. We can use discussion groups to encourage virtual discussions outside of class, or even schedule live chats for the same purpose. Students can create web pages instead of (or in addition to) writing term papers.

With the advent of the Internet also came the opportunity to offer courses completely on-line. Students can earn degrees from anywhere in the world, as long as they have access to a computer. While this method is not practical for every discipline (imagine holding organic chemistry lab on-line), many others have found it to be a convenient and rewarding experience.

Some colleges and universities have the benefit of software programs that allow all these functions to exist in one location. Blackboard software is especially useful for this purpose, and is even used in some settings to manage virtual courses.

Even those of you who do not yet have access to Internet course management software can use the applications discussed in Chapter 1 to supplement your courses.

Using Web Pages

Creating a Course Web Page

Why create a web page for your course? Well, think of it as the "command center" of the class itself. When students have access to a class web page, they can download the syllabus or assignments at any time without having to bother the instructor or teaching assistants. Students can quickly recall dates for exams or pull up homework assignments they missed—if you choose to allow them to do that.

Other applications of course web pages include relevant links for each lecture—Internet applications can be listed for each individual lecture, if you decide to include such detail on the page. Finally, you can include a list of textbooks with links to local bookstores.

Creating your own course web page is as easy as creating a document in a word processor. Even if you do not receive course web space from your university (unlikely at the writing of this Appendix, but possible), you can use the free services discussed in Chapter 1 to set up a course web page.

Student Web Pages

You may have your students set up a topical web site for class. Encourage them to create a site devoted to something they feel strongly about in criminal justice. For example, they may be interested in creating a page dedicated to the issue of domestic violence. They can provide links to relevant web sites and even their own papers written on the subject.

Of course, having them complete this assignment does no good if others don't visit the site. Perhaps as an additional assignment, have other students in the class visit their classmates' sites and provide critiques. Or, hold a contest for the best web site created specifically for the course. You can also link to these sites from the course web page to encourage students to put sufficient time and effort into the projects.

Using Multimedia in the Classroom

I have found it extremely useful to display web pages in the classroom. Informational web sites are useful in the classroom, but the most helpful sites contain movies and images that help illustrate your points. At the very least, using these resources helps to break up lecture and keep students interested.

As an example, I frequently teach a course in research methods in criminal justice. An essential section of this course covers research ethics, and we typically discuss controversial research projects. These typically include Milgram's "electric shock" experiment, Humphries' "Tearoom Trade", and the Stanford Prison Study. It is sometimes difficult for students to relate to these projects and how they were actually done. Philip Zimbardo has created an outstanding web resource at *http://www.zimbardo.com/prison.htm*. This site contains images and movie footage from the study. In my experience, this helps students become involved and interested in research rather than just reading about it in a textbook.

Unfortunately, not all of you have the resources to use the Internet in the classroom. Colleges and universities are increasingly adding technology classrooms to their campuses, but at some places this growth is very slow. Be sure to let your computer center know that you would like to have the opportunity to use new technology in the classroom!

Course Discussions

Many courses include grades for class discussion, but there are always students who are uncomfortable speaking in front of a large group. Having electronic discussions allows all students to speak their mind without embarrassment. If in-class discussions are mandatory for your students, "virtual" discussions can be used as extra credit or to supplement material covered in class.

E-mail

I do not have to describe the benefits of email to most of you reading this Appendix. E-mail facilitates communication between faculty and students—they can find you even when you are not in the office, and you can reply at your leisure. One of the most useful applications of e-mail in the classroom is the ability to use mailing lists to communicate with your students and keep them informed.

Mailing Lists

At our university, criminal justice students can sign up for the criminal justice mailing list and receive information about new courses, internship, job opportunities, and other items relevant to them. As with other mailing lists, this can be received as individual emails (list mode) or one message with several emails (digest mode). For example, I received a message from the mailing list today that begins:

There are 4 messages totaling 320 lines in this issue.

Topics of the day:

1. Attention Graduate Students: Upcoming Workshops
2. Tutors Wanted
3. Professional Panel Discussion by the Economic Crime Council

****
Topic #1:

ATTENTION GRADUATE AND PhD STUDENTS. Following are important upcoming workshops that you may be interested in attending. If you have any questions, please contact the department that is sponsoring the event you are interested in.

> UCRIHS SEMINAR for Graduate Students, Post-Docs,
> and Research Associates (UCRIHS University
> Committee on Research Involving Human Subjects)

(Remainder of email message omitted)

****
Topic #2:
> If you enjoy helping others, have strong leadership
> skills, or are good at explaining subject matter,
> then we have the perfect position for you. The
> Learning Resources Center is looking for tutors for
> the fall 2002 school year. Tutors are needed in
> the following areas:
>
> Accounting
> Economics
> Math/Statistics
> Chemistry

(Remainder of digest omitted)

The benefit of receiving these updates in digest mode is clear—messages are grouped together so as not to overload your email inbox if many messages are sent in one day.

A mailing list is best used for class announcements and other news that does not need to be discussed. As you can guess, a discussion can be difficult to follow when people are responding to many emails at once. For that reason, class discussions are best done in a discussion group or Usenet. Contact your computer center for information about creating a mailing list for your course.

Discussion Groups and Usenet

If your goal for your students is to engage in class discussions on-line, then a discussion group is perfect for this task (hence the name!). Usenet groups can be created through your college or university's computer center. Several courses at Michigan State have Usenet groups dedicated to class that are only accessible by those with MSU privileges. However, all individuals with MSU computer privileges can access Usenet groups, so you should consider how important it is to keep your group restricted to class members. Once the group is created, students can use special software to access the Newsgroup (such as Outlook Express or Xnews).

You can start a discussion group without help from your computer center if you use one of the freely available groups at MSN or Yahoo! Groups. There are many other opportunities to begin groups—it just takes some creative searching of the Internet. Once a group is created, you can invite students to participate and begin discussion!

As an example, here's a discussion group I created in Yahoo! Groups for my undergraduate research methods course:

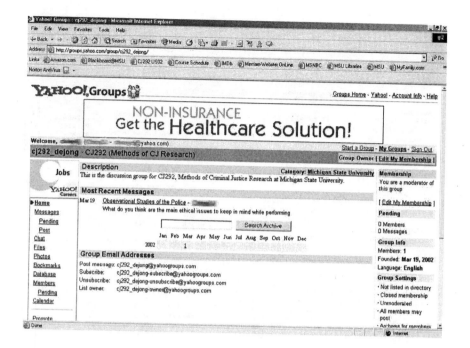

Chat

If your preference is to schedule a live chat for your students, services such as IRC, ICQ, or even AOL & MSN can be used for chat purposes. See the detailed FAQs available for these services in Chapter One.

Using mIRC, I have opened a chat room for my students to discuss the issue of police brutality. The IRC server we are currently using is Sorcery, or irc.sorcery.net (Port 9000). If you choose to use mIRC, you can select from a predetermined list of IRC servers. All you need to do is select one, then let you students know the location. You can create a channel by typing:

/join #death_penalty

where #death_penalty is the name of the channel for discussion. Here's a sample of the class in the midst of discussion:

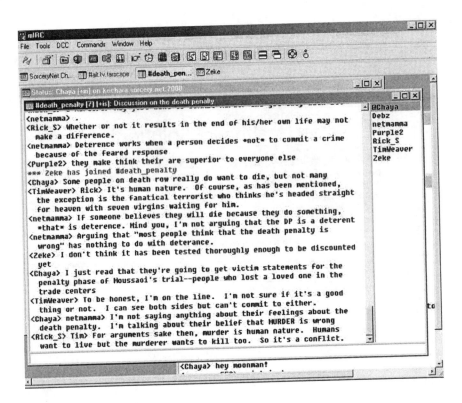

Some of you may be wondering why we use the Internet for discussion as opposed to live discussions in the classroom. The first reason is simple—on-line discussion does not have to replace classroom discussion. As with any course supplement, on-line discussion can help add to the learning experience. Classroom discussion is vital, but students will sometimes have good ideas for discussion after class has ended. Scheduling an on-line chat (whether live or via a discussion board) allows students to express their opinions after they have had time to digest the material and think about the issue at hand.

Another benefit of on-line chat is that it encourages shy or hesitant students to participate in a way that may be more comfortable for them. I frequently have students who will not participate in classroom chats for those very reasons. When they are able to engage in "virtual" discussions, they can demonstrate keen insights into course material. Internet discussion gives them an opportunity to participate that they might not have in class. In addition, these students sometimes become more comfortable as the term progresses, and your positive feedback about their performance may help them overcome insecurities about speaking in front of others.

Finally, it may be more convenient to hold discussions on controversial topics if you allow students to post and/or chat anonymously. Students are sometimes hesitant to become involved in discussions on these kinds of topics.

However, allowing students to post or chat anonymously may cause problems. There may be students in your class who abuse their chat or email privileges by harassing other students or using profanity. Use your best judgment to decide whether you can trust your students to post responsibly.

File Transfer

Like most businesses, colleges and universities are replacing paper documents with electronic documents. At Michigan State University, for example, hard copies of course schedules are no longer available—all information about courses offered is found on-line. These sources are more dynamic than old paper sources—they can include current enrollment figures and instructor changes can be updated continuously (future students may not understand jokes about how many courses "Professor STAFF" teaches at the University).

You can encourage your students to turn in documents electronically by allowing file transfer, either through Email or FTP. The advantages of allowing students to submit electronically include:

- Easy transport of many documents (instead of carrying home a large stack of papers, you can carry home a small stack of floppy disks or one zip disk).
- It is very difficult to lose electronic copies of files. Even if the file is accidentally deleted from your folder, the student will have a backup copy.
- You can be sure that the work was done prior to the due date, since each file will have the date & time submitted.

- Word Processors allow you to insert comments and make changes quite easily. They can be inserted in a different color so students can pick out your changes from the regular text.

The advantages of electronic submission for students are:

- Easily readable comments by professors—no need to translate written comments "back into" English (personally, the longer I teach the worse my handwriting becomes).
- Lost papers become a thing of the past. When papers were written on typewriters, students rarely kept a copy of their work. When the have to submit papers electronically, they are forced to save an electronic copy that is conveniently time and date stamped.
- Economy—you're saving money for yourself, your school, and your students if they don't have to print every assignment for your course.

Summary

This chapter has demonstrated some of the advantages of using the Internet for criminal justice research. A course home page can create a central "communication center" for students and the instructor, as well as a repository for course documents. In addition, e-mail and discussion groups help to facilitate class discussions after class has ended. Luckily for us and for our students, resources for teaching and learning are increasing at an exponential rate. Keep your eyes open for new and innovative technology, and think creatively! (And let me know if you find something REALLY cool.)

Appendix B
Uniform Resource Locator (URL) Index

This index contains all URLs discussed in the text, organized by chapter. All general criminal justice links (such as those used in examples) can be found at the each of each chapter's section.

Chapter One: What is the Internet?

Using the Web

A Guide to URLs
> *http://www.netspace.org/users/dwb/url-guide.html*

Domain listing
> *http://www.iana.org/cctld/cctld-whois.htm*

Internet Tools Summary
> *http://www.december.com/net/tools*

Hypertext Markup Language (HTML)

A Beginner's Guide to HTML
> *http://www.msg.net/tutorial/html-primer.html*

HTML Help
> *http://www.obscure.org/~jaws/htmlhelp.html*

The Almost Complete HTML reference
> *http://www.computronics.be/courses/htmlcourse/otherinfo/specs.html*

Free Web Space

Yahoo! Geocities
  http://yahoo.geocities.com

Search Engines

Search.com
  http://www.search.com
Switchboard
  http://www.switchboard.com

Usenet and Newsreaders

Basic Information on Usenet
  http://www.smr-usenet.com/
Google Groups
  http://groups.google.com
The Net: User Guidelines and Netiquette
  http://www.fau.edu/netiquette

Chat

IRC (Internet Relay Chat)
  http://www.irchelp.org
ICQ (I Seek You)
  http://www.icq.com
mIRC (Software to use IRC)
  http://www.mirc.com

Getting Help

On-line Internet Guide
  http://www.December.com/net/tools

Criminal Justice Links

Federal Bureau of Investigation
http://www.fbi.gov
FBI Uniform Crime Reports
http://www.fbi.gov/ucr/ucr.htm
New York City Police Department
http://www.nyc.gov/html/nypd/home.html
The Central Intelligence Agency
http://www.cia.gov/
CIA Frequently Asked Questions
http://www.cia.gov/cia/public_affairs/faq.html

Chapter Two: Internet Applications in Criminal Justice

News & Events

The Japan Times
http://www.japantimes.co.jp/
The Times (UK)
http://www.thetimes.co.uk/
The New York Times
http://www.nytimes.com/
The Chicago Tribune
http://www.Chicago.tribune.com/
The Washington Post
http://www.washingtonpost.com/
The Los Angeles Times
http://www.latimes.com/
College Newspaper Sites
http://www.collegenews.com/campusnews.htm

CNN
http://www.cnn.com
MSNBC
http://www.msnbc.com

Fox News
   http://www.foxnews.com

National Public Radio
   http://www.npr.org/
Live Internet Radio
   http://www.live-radio.net/

Journals and Books

Amazon
   http://www.amazon.com
Barnes & Noble
   http://www.barnesandnoble.com
Journal of Criminal Justice and Popular Culture
   http://www.albany.edu/scj/jcjpc/

Criminal Justice Links

COPS office
   http://www.usdoj.gov/cops/
The Police Foundation
   http://www.policefoundation.org/
National Center for Community Policing
   http://cj.msu.edu/~people/cp/

CrimeTheory.com
   http://www.crimetheory.com
Critical Criminology
   http://www.critcrim.org
American Society of Criminology
   http://www.asc41.org
Australian Institute of Criminology
   http://www.aic.gov.au/
Korean Institute of Criminology
   http://www.kic.re.kr/
   http://www.kic.re.kr/eng/e_main.php (English language version)

Scandinavian Research Council for Criminology
http://www.nsfk.org/

Vera Institute of Justice
http://www.vera.org
RAND Corporation
http://www.rand.org/crim
Institute for Law and Justice
http://www.ilj.org

American Civil Liberties Union
http://www.aclu.org/issues/criminal/hmcj.html
Center for Rational Correctional Policy
http://www.correctionalpolicy.com
Families Against Mandatory Minimums
http://www.famm.org
"Anatomy of a Murder"
http://www.library.thinkquest.org/2760/homep.htm

Chapter Three: Using the Internet for Criminal Justice Research

Resources for Internet Research

Yahoo!
http://www.yahoo.com
Google
http://www.google.com
Excite
http://www.excite.com
Iwon
http://www.iwon.com

Downloadable Data

The Sourcebook of Criminal Justice Statistics
http://www.albany.edu/sourcebook
The Uniform Crime Reports
http://www.fbi.gov/ucr/ucr.htm
The National Archive of Criminal Justice Data
http://www.icpsr.umich.edu/NACJD

Criminal Justice Links

Bureau of Alcohol, Tobacco and Firearms
http://www.atf.treas.gov/
Death Penalty Information Center
http://www.deathpenaltyinfo.org/
Texas Department of Criminal Justice, Death Row Information
http://www.tdcj.state.tx.us/stat/deathrow.htm
Bureau of Justice Statistics
http://www.ojp.usdoj.gov/bjs/welcome.html

Chapter Four: Criminal Justice Careers and the Internet

Career Aids On-line

Bureau of Labor Statistics, Occupational Outlook Handbook
http://www.bls.gov/oco
Career Planning
http://www.careerplanning.org/
Job Web
http://www.jobweb.com
Résumé writing
http://www.resume-cover-letter.info
Interviewing
http://www.ocs.fas.harvard.edu/html/intview.html

USAJOBS
http://www.usajobs.opm.gov
Hot Jobs
http://www.hotjobs.com
Monster
http://www.monster.com

Criminal Justice Links

Dallas Police Department
http://www.dallaspolice.net
Tarrant County Sheriff's Department
http://www.tarrantcounty.com/sheriff/site/default.asp
Texas Department of Public Safety
http://www.txdps.state.tx.us